PAKISTAN

MAJOR WORLD NATIONS

PAKISTAN

John C. Caldwell

CHELSEA HOUSE PUBLISHERS
Philadelphia

Chelsea House Publishers

Copyright © 2000 by Chelsea House Publishers,
a division of Main Line Book Co.
All rights reserved.
Printed in Malaysia

First Printing.

1 3 5 7 9 8 6 4 2

Library of Congress Cataloging-in-Publication Data

Caldwell, John C. (John Cope), 1913-
Pakistan / John C. Caldwell.
p.   cm. — (Major world nations)
Includes index.
Summary: Describes the geography, history, religious life, people, and daily
life of the border country between Iran and Afghanistan.
ISBN 0-7910-5392-X (hc)
1. Pakistan—Juvenile literature. [1. Pakistan.] I. Caldwell,
John C. (John Cope), 1913- Let's visit Pakistan. II. Title.
III. Series
DS376.9.C35   1999
954.91—dc21   99-11827
CIP

ACKNOWLEDGEMENTS

The Author and Publishers are grateful to the following organizations and individuals
for permission to reproduce copyright photographs in this book:
D.A.F.P.; Douglas Dickens; The Government of Pakistan; I.C.A.;
Keystone Press Agency; Paul Popper Ltd.; Torge Photos; U.S.I.S.

CONTENTS

PAKISTAN
and her Neighbours

AFGHANISTAN
PAKISTAN
KASHMIR
CHINA
TIBET
NEPAL
INDIA
BANGLADESH
ARABIAN SEA
SRI LANKA

MILES
0   500
KILOMETRES
0   800

Main map:

CHINA

KHYBER PASS
Peshawar
KASHMIR
Kabul
Srinagar
Islamabad
Rawalpindi
Jhelum
Jammu
HIMALAYA MTS.
R.Chenab
Sialkot
R.Jhelum
Lahore
R.Beas
AFGHANISTAN
R.Indus
R.Ravi
Quetta
Multan
PUNJAB
BALUCHISTAN
R.Indus
R.Sutlej
PAKISTAN
GREAT INDIAN DESERT
IRAN
Mohenjo-Daro RUINS
INDIA
Karachi
Hyderabad
SIND

ARABIAN SEA

MILES
0   500
KILOMETRES
0   800

FACTS AT A GLANCE

Land and People

Official Name	Islamic Republic of Pakistan
Location	Southern Asia
Area	350,000 square miles (888,000 square kilometers)
Climate	Varies–dry and hot in the deserts; cold in the mountains; temperate in the valleys
Capital	Islamadad
Other Cities	Karachi, Lahore, Faisalabad, Gilgit, Peshawar, Ormara
Population	135 million
Population Distribution	Urban, 33 percent; rural, 67 percent
Major Rivers	Indus, Jhelum, Chenab, Ravi, Beas, Sutlej
Mountains	Himalayan, Hindu Kush, Karakoram
Official Language	Urdu, English
Other Languages	Punjabi, Sindhi, Saraiki, Pahtu, Balochi, Hindko, Brahni

8

Ethnic Groups	Punjabi, Sindhi, Pashtun, Baloch, Muhajir
Religions	Islam, 97 percent (Sunni, 77 percent; Shi'a, 20 percent); Christian, 2 percent; Hindu and other, 1 percent
Literacy Rate	37.8 percent
Average Life Expectancy	59.07 years

Economy

Natural Resources	Natural gas, petroleum, coal, iron ore, copper, salt, limestone
Division of Labor Force	Agriculture, 47 percent; mining and manufacturing, 17 percent; services, 17 percent
Agricultural Products	Cotton, wheat, rice, sugarcane, fruits, vegetables, dairy products, beef
Industries	Textiles, food processing, paper products, clothing, construction materials
Major Imports	Petroleum and petroleum products, machinery, transportation equipment, chemicals
Major Exports	Cotton, textiles, clothing, rice, carpets
Currency	Rupee

Government

Form of Government	Federal republic
Government Bodies	National Assembly, Senate
Formal Head of State	President
Head of Government	Prime minister

HISTORY AT A GLANCE

2500-1500 B.C.   The people living in the Indus valley begin to build large, well-planned cities and create their own alphabet.. Around 1500 B.C. this great Indus valley civilization suddenly vanishes.

1500-500 B.C.   Aryan nomads travel through the Khyber Pass and into the Indus valley. A written language is developed called Sanskrit.

6th century B.C.   The Persian king, Darius, invades the subcontinent (as the area comprising India and Pakistan is called) and makes the northwestern portion part of his empire.

326 B.C.   Alexander the Great invades India and the Greek and Indian armies fight on the banks of the Jhelum River.

**3rd century B.C.–
6th century A.D.**   Various invaders come to the area, take over the land, and eventually are overcome by other invaders. Some of the invaders come from Persia, Afghanistan, Central Asia, and Greece. The two religions of Hinduism and Buddhism both thrive with most people in the area that would become Pakistan practicing Hinduism.

712-998 A.D.	Arabs invade the area of present-day Pakistan, defeat the Hindu king, and take over the land. They introduce the Muslim religion to the area.
998	Amir Sabuktigin and his army raid the area beginning what will be a series of raids from central Asia. Thousands of Hindus are killed in the battles that ensue.
1175-1200	The Muslim warrior Mohammed Ghori conquers all of the area that today comprises Pakistan and northern India.
1200-1525	The Muslims rule the area for over three centuries. Their religion spreads and Hindus are persecuted and made to pay special taxes.
1525	Muslim Turks under Babur take over the area and begin the great Mogul dynasty of India.
1556-1605	Babur's grandson, Akbar the Great, takes over the throne. He abolishes the restrictions on the Hindus and preaches tolerance for all religions. His kingdom eventually includes all of the subcontinent and the area prospers under his rule.
1707-1858	The Mogul dynasty gradually collapses and India becomes divided into smaller kingdoms.
1757-1900	The British and the British East India Company gradually gain a stronghold throughout the subcontinent.
1857-1858	First War for Independence is fought by Muslims. They are defeated and the last emperor of the Mogul Dynasty is forced to leave the country.

1909 Mohammed Ali Jinnah is elected to the Imperial Legislative Council and works unceasingly for Hindu-Muslim unity as the lifeline of the country.

1930 Jinnah finally realizes that there could never be unity between the two great religions and leads the struggle for two separate countries—one Muslim, one Hindi.

1947 After years of negotiations, on August 14 Britain officially gives India its independence and the two nations of India and Pakistan are born.

1948 On January 30, the revered Indian leader, Gandhi, is assassinated and in their horror Pakistan and india finally negotiate without bloodshed.

1949 The United Nations arranges a cease-fire between India and Pakistan who had been fighting over ownership of Kashmir.

1951 The overwhelming problems of Pakistan being divided into two separate parts, East and West, with over 1,000 miles between them become more and more evident.

1958 After years of political upheaval and tensions between East Pakistan and West Pakistan, General Ayub Khan takes over the government and declares martial law.

1965 National elections are held for the first time in 17 years and Khan is officially elected president for another term.

1972 After years of tension and conflict between East and West Pakistan, a brief and bitter war is fought and East Pakistan declares itself an independent country named Bangladesh.

12

1972-1977	Zulfikar Ali Bhutto is prime minister of Pakistan. He makes large strides in organizing the country.
1977-1985	Riots following elections cause a military takeover with General Zia-ul-haq heading the government. Marital law is declared.
1985	General Zia lifts the martial law and allows elections for a National Assembly.
1988	Zia is killed in a plane crash. Elections are held and Benazir Bhutto becomes prime minister. She is the first woman to head a modern Muslim country.
1990	Bhutto is accused of corruption and a new election is held in which a Punjab prime minister is elected, Mian Nawaz Sharif.
1993	Sharif's government is also accused of corruption and Bhutto is re-elected. Economic problems continue to cripple the country and the literacy rate is only 25 percent. The United States accuses Pakistan of violating international arms agreements by buying weapons and weapon technology from China.
1996	Bhutto is dismissed as prime minister by President Farooq Leghari because of charges of corruption, decline in law and order, and economic mismanagement. Malik Meraj Khalid is appointed acting prime minister.
1997	Elections are held and Sharif is again elected prime minister with an overwhelming majority. He faces dismal economic conditions and continued strong political opposition.
1998	Pakistan's testing of a nuclear weapon shocks the world.

13

A Pakistani shepherd boy.

1

Let's Visit Pakistan

Pakistan is one of the several new countries in the continent of Asia. It occupies a little more than one-sixth of the Indian subcontinent. Until 1947 most of the Indian subcontinent was a single country under British rule. Then it became two countries, independent of Britain and of each other. One of the two, the vast central and southern area, kept the name India. The other, carved out of what had been northeast and northwest India, took the new name Pakistan.

This meant that Pakistan was divided into two separate sections. Both were under the same government, even though they were over 1,000 miles (over 1,600 kilometers) apart by land or air, and even further apart by sea. If a citizen of West Pakistan traveled to East Pakistan by sea, his voyage covered some 3,000 miles (about 4,800 kilometers), or the distance across the Atlantic Ocean. This wide division made it difficult for the people of the two sections to think of themselves as one nation. An even greater difficulty was that they spoke different languages, had different surroundings and interests, ate different food, and even looked different.

Why, then, were they expected to become one nation? The official name of the country—The Islamic Republic of Pakistan—gives a clue to the reason. Islam is the proper name for what we often call Mohammedanism, the religion established by Mohammed. Believers in this religion are called Muslims or Mohammedans. Islam is the religion of most Arab people who live in the Middle East. It is also the religion of many of the people of North Africa, Indonesia, and several other countries. Those other countries include Pakistan. In 1947, Pakistan had the largest population of

Islam is the official religion of Pakistan. This picture, taken in Karachi, shows Muslim worshippers who have removed their shoes for prayer in accordance with custom.

Muslims in the world. So it was hoped that the common religion would bridge the many differences between the country's two sections. However, the differences proved too wide for bridging. In 1971, East Pakistan broke away from West Pakistan, to become the independent country of Bangladesh, leaving the old western section as the only Pakistan. That is the Pakistan of today, the country we are visiting. Let's look at the map and find out more clearly where we are.

About 120 miles (200 kilometers) from the Tropic of Cancer, Pakistan faces the Arabian Sea, which forms its southern boundary. It is bounded on the west by Iran (Persia) and on the north by Afghanistan. In the extreme north, a small part of it comes quite close to China. The entire eastern border adjoins India and the territory of Kashmir.

Within these boundaries Pakistan has about 310,000 square miles (800,000 square kilometers) of land which is mainly dry. Rainfall averages from about four to 25 inches (10 to 64 centimeters) a year, most of it falling in July, August, and September. On the coast the weather is usually warm and often very hot. On the inland plains it is very hot in summer and extremely cold in winter. In summer the temperature may sometimes rise as high as 122 degrees Fahrenheit (50 degrees Celsius) during the day and rarely falls below 90 degrees Fahrenheit (32 degrees Celsius) at night. But in the winter, although the temperature may reach 70 degrees Fahrenheit (21 degrees Celsius) during the day, it often falls to freezing-point at night.

The largest river of Pakistan, the Indus, rises in the Tibetan

Plateau and is 1,700 miles (2,700 kilometers) long. The Indus is among the most important rivers in Asia. It is especially important to Pakistan, for it flows the whole length of the country, emptying into the Arabian Sea.

Karachi, the former capital and an important seaport, is located near the mouth of the Indus. The Indus and its tributaries provide Pakistan with its water supply. Although rainfall is as low as four inches (10 centimeters) a year in some areas, the river valley soil is rich and fine crops can be grown. The central area of Pakistan is called the Punjab which means "Land of Five Rivers." You will see that five large tributaries—namely the Jhelum, Chenab, Ravi, Beas, and Sutlej—flow in a southerly direction before finally uniting to join the Indus. These rivers are connected by long stretches of canal. Some of these canals were built thousands of years ago.

A scene in Kashmir.

A Pakistani farmer planting cotton. It is difficult to believe that anything could grow in this sun-baked ground—but it does.

At some points there are huge dams to store the water. The precious water from the Indus and the five rivers makes the Punjab fertile.

There are fields of wheat and cotton, and in some areas there is sufficient water to grow rice.

You will see on the map that some of these important rivers flow through both India and Pakistan. As both countries need plenty of water to grow their crops, it was thought essential at the time of partition in 1947 that the waters of these rivers should be fairly divided. Otherwise, unpleasant disputes might arise.

So, under the auspices of the International Bank for Recon-

Fishermen in Baluchistan making ropes from palm leaves.

Baluchi nomads.

struction and Development, the water rights of the Indus system of rivers were settled by the signing of the Indus Water Treaty. This treaty was signed by both Pakistan and India on September 19, 1960.

Broadly speaking, the waters of the three eastern rivers—the Sutlej, Beas, and Ravi—are reserved for Indian use and development. The waters of the Chenab, Jhelum, and Indus, with its tributaries, are available to Pakistan.

A huge system of dams and canals was needed to replace the waters from the eastern rivers, which formerly irrigated the Punjab and Sind areas of Pakistan. The work has recently been finished and Pakistan has one of the world's longest irrigation systems.

Away from the rivers the land is dry and rocky. To the east, the Thar or Indian Desert forms a huge tract along the borders of Pakistan and India. West of the Indus, there is flat desert land which leads into dry, rocky hills. This western area, bordering

A Baluchi woman from the border country between Iran and Afghanistan. Note her beautiful ornaments; she is wearing a nose-ring as other women might wear earrings.

A camel train crossing a mountain watercourse. Note the snow-capped peaks in the background, typical of some of Pakistan's most beautiful regions.

Iran and Afghanistan, is called Baluchistan. *Istan* means "the land of" in Persian. Just as Pakistan means "Land of the Pure," *Baluchistan* means "Land of the Baluchi People" and *Afghanistan* means "Land of the Afghans."

Thus, most of Pakistan is a land of deserts, rocky hills and, in some areas, beautiful snowcapped mountains. There are oases scattered through the desert, but extensive farming is possible only near the Indus River and its tributaries where there are many irrigation projects and a system of canals which makes it possible for the otherwise dry land to be farmed.

The highest mountains of Pakistan, called the Hindu Kush, lie along the northern part of the Pakistan-Afghanistan border. Mount Tirich Mir is 25,230 feet (about 7,700 meters) high, and the Istoro Nal is over 24,000 feet (about 7,300 meters).

The deserts, dry hills, and mountains along its western border cut Pakistan off from its neighbors. There are only a few passes through which people can travel safely and easily. One of these, called the Khyber Pass, has often been the gateway for invaders who have conquered the Indian subcontinent. The sides of this famous pass are spiked with fortifications, some built centuries ago.

The Khyber Pass begins at a place called Jamrud, about 11 miles (18 kilometers) from Peshawar. It then twists and turns for over 33 miles (54 kilometers) until it reaches an outpost called Dakha.

Through this fateful pass over the centuries the Persians, the Greeks, the Tartars, the Turks, and the Afghans all entered India

Some parts of Pakistan are desert. These tribesmen, performing a traditional stick dance in Baluchistan, seem not to notice the intense desert heat.

Using bullocks to harvest rice in Sind, one of Pakistan's four provinces.

in turn. They toppled weak empires and founded new dynasties, and left permanent marks on the history of the subcontinent.

Rudyard Kipling, one of the most popular English writers of the late 19th century, lived in Pakistan when it was a part of the British colony of India. Several of Kipling's poems tell of battles in the Khyber Pass, or describe the wild mountain tribes who lived nearby. Later we shall learn more about the invading armies which came through the pass. The rough dry territory into which they descended is now Pakistan's Northwest Frontier Province, one of the six government areas into which the country is divided. Four of the six—the Northwest Frontier, Punjab, Baluchistan, and Sind—are provinces, each with its own local government. The other two are administered by the national government, from the

25

A view of Islamabad—Pakistan's capital built on meadowland in the northern part of the country.

newly-built capital Islamabad. Though the national language is Urdu (a language brought to the Indian subcontinent by Muslim invaders) some of these areas have languages of their own. For instance, the people of the Punjab speak Punjabi, the people of Sind speak Sindhi, and so forth.

26

Most Pakistanis are light-skinned, like this mountain boy.

However, most of the 135,000,000 Pakistanis share the same distant ancestors in spite of their different languages. They are of Aryan stock, descendants of a powerful, light-skinned people who came through the Khyber Pass in ancient times. Many Indians are also of Aryan stock. So how is it that two nations with a common ancestry and many common problems can be as different as Pakistan and India? As we shall learn, religion is the greatest dividing factor, and was the reason for the geographical and political division. While Pakistan is predominantly Muslim, India is predominantly Hindu. Religion has probably been the most important single factor in Pakistan's long and unusual history. This history begins in the mysteries of a civilization which existed almost 5,000 years ago.

2

The Mysterious Past

Our picture shows an ancient city, discovered by archaeologists not many years ago. This city is named Mohenjo-Daro, which means "Mound of the Dead." It is located in the Indus valley, 267 miles (425 kilometers) inland from Karachi. Other similar cities and towns have been unearthed all along the Indus valley.

We have no name for the builders of Mohenjo-Daro, other than "the Indus valley people." We do not know whether they were white, brown, or black. It is possible that these people were the

The ruins of Mohenjo-Daro, a great city built 4,000 years ago.

first to use an alphabet. Many of their inscriptions have been found, but so far scientists have been unable to decipher the writing. Even the exact date when the Indus valley people existed is unknown. Their great cities were probably built between 2500 and 1500 B.C., or about 4,000 years ago.

These Indus valley cities were large and well-built. There were numerous two-story houses. The larger houses had many rooms, including bathrooms. The streets were wide and paved, and most of the buildings were of brick.

These unknown people of Pakistan's remote past had also discovered and used metals; objects made of copper, lead and silver were found in the buried cities. Metal tools have been unearthed, too, as well as ornamental objects.

The manner in which the ancient cities of the Indus valley are built shows that the people were good engineers. The cities are well-planned. They have drainage systems and, even after centuries, we can see that the drains were kept clean. It would appear that the Indus valley cities even had street-cleaning departments!

These vanished people were fine craftsmen. They made figurines and carvings which show elephants, tigers, and oxen. The greatest unsolved mystery about them is the distinctive writing carved into pots and on the official seals which must have been used by the government. Many archaeologists have tried to read this script, but the writing is unlike that of any other ancient people.

In fact, even the houses, the tools, and the clothing worn by the Indus valley people are different from those of any other ancient civilization. So many of their cities and villages have been found that we know that there were a good many of these people—perhaps several million. We also know, from the fine buildings and the big granaries where grain was stored, that the Indus valley was a land of great wealth.

Some archaeologists believe that the Indus valley people must have come into what is now Pakistan from some other part of the world. One reason for this belief is that they used metals which are not found in the Indus valley. In addition, they cultivated wheat and raised sheep; but the wheat came from wild grasses, and the sheep from wild sheep, both found only in mountainous areas far distant from the Indus.

There were other large cities in addition to Mohenjo-Daro. Among them was Harappa in the Punjab. There was also a more recently discovered city at Kot Diji. They enjoyed a high civilization for many years. Then, suddenly, the bustling life of these cities came to a stop. We do not know exactly when this happened; but, just as mysteriously as the Indus valley civilization began, it disappeared. Archaeologists believe that whatever happened to bring this civilization to an end occurred in about 1500 B.C.

Some scientists think there may have been a great plague that wiped out the population. Or, more probably, invaders came, killed all the people and moved elsewhere. We may never know the answer to this mystery. We only know that one of the greatest of ancient civilizations suddenly vanished. The Indus valley people died, or were killed, or perhaps moved elsewhere. The great cities were covered by drifting sand, and it is only within the past

A typical farm village in Pakistan. The oxen are valuable beasts of burden.

60 years that they have been dug up. Perhaps some day someone will unlock the secret of the Indus valley by learning to read the script.

Although the people disappeared, some of their achievements lived through the dark ages that followed. The village carts used in parts of Pakistan today are the same, even to the wheel-span, as those of the Indus valley people. Village potters in modern Pakistan use designs similar to those created by the ancient potters of the Indus.

After the Indus valley civilization disappeared, there was a blank period which lasted for centuries. By this we mean that there are no records to tell us what happened. There are no remains to tell us anything about the people who probably conquered the Indus cities.

It is possible that many invaders came through the Khyber Pass during these centuries. But the first ones about whom we have any facts were the Aryans. It is known that these people began to pour into what is now Pakistan in about 1500 B.C.

The coming of these invaders brings us to the next period of Pakistan's history. This period is one shared by India. During the centuries following the first known invasion from outside, there were no differences between the people of the Indian subcontinent: everyone believed in the religion established by the newcomers, and all people followed similar customs.

3

Invaders from the North

In about 1500 B.C., wandering tribes from Central Asia and the borderlands between Europe and Asia began to come into the land we know as Pakistan. It is probable that most of these people traveled through the Khyber Pass and into the flat lands along the Indus River. This pass is one of the few ways of crossing the mountains which separate Pakistan and Afghanistan. It cuts through the Sofed Koh Mountains. The invasions continued for 1,000 years.

The Khyber Pass, through which countless invading armies have poured; it has played a crucial role in the history of the Indian subcontinent.

The newcomers were tall and fair-skinned. They were related to the Greeks, the Persians, and the later Romans; and they belonged to the Aryan branch of the human family.

The Aryan nomads spread through what is now Pakistan and moved steadily eastward into the plains of northern India. There were already dark-skinned people called Dravidians living in India. The Aryans drove the Dravidians southward. Sometimes the Dravidians became slaves of the conquerors; at other times relations were peaceful. Many Dravidians still live in southern India.

The invasions from the north came in waves. Sometimes a new wave of Aryans would conquer others who had arrived many years earlier.

In about 518 B.C. a great Persian king called Darius crossed the Himalayan passes and invaded the subcontinent. He made the northwestern portion of India a part of his empire.

Two centuries later, in 326 B.C., Alexander the Great began his campaign in India. A great battle was fought between the Greek and Indian armies on the banks of the Jhelum River. The Indian King Porus was completely defeated. Alexander, encouraged by his victory, advanced as far as the Beas River. But his soldiers were weary and homesick; they yearned for Greece. So Alexander had to turn back. With his return, the Greek rule in northern India ended.

After Alexander's death, the Persians invaded again; they were followed by other people known as Scythians and Kushans. But the dry lands which we know as Pakistan were not as attractive to the newcomers as were the more fertile plains of India. So, while many did settle in what is now Pakistan, many others moved on. In the plains of northern India, the Aryans established many kingdoms and a number of dynasties of Indian or Hindu kings. Remember that at this time, and for centuries to come, India and Pakistan were one.

They were followed by the kings of the Maurya Dynasty—the first powerful line of Hindu kings. Their greatest king was Asoka, who came to power in 274 B.C. For hundreds of years the pattern of history in the Indian subcontinent repeated itself. There would be a powerful dynasty, controlling much of the land; then there would be revolts and war and the founding of smaller, independent kingdoms. The smaller kingdoms would last until the next powerful ruler came to conquer them.

The most important development of this period was that of the Hindu religion and way of life. We know that religion was to become the great divider in the formation of modern Pakistan and India. It is important for us to know something about Hinduism because the main difference between a modern Pakistani and a citizen of modern India is that of religion.

The Aryan invaders developed a written language called Sanskrit. Twelve of the 14 most important languages of India were developed from this ancient language. Furthermore, Bengali—the language of Bangladesh—is also derived from Sanskrit.

Through the centuries, the beliefs of Hinduism were written down in Sanskrit in a series of holy books called the Vedas. There are numerous other Hindu books, too, some in the form

Selling dates in a local market in Pakistan.

of poetry, which tell stories of Aryan conquest and which helped to make the Hindu beliefs a vital part of the life of the people. What are these beliefs which have lasted until modern times?

Hindus believe in one Creator, a god whose name is Brahma. There are numerous other Hindu gods, the most important and powerful of them being Vishnu the Preserver, and Shiva the Destroyer. A Hindu worships these and many other gods. He believes that life is filled with evil, and that before attaining perfection a man must be reborn again and again. We call this "reincarnation." As each life is lived, a little of the evil may disappear until, at last, perfection has been achieved. This process might take hundreds of years. At some stage during the many lives, a man might be a lowly farmer, be reborn as a merchant, and eventually become a priest or nobleman.

Another important Hindu belief, taught in the Vedas, or sacred books, is that certain animals, especially cattle, are sacred. A good Hindu will eat no meat at all; it is only in very modern times that Hindus have ever eaten beef.

36

Remember that when the proud and warlike Aryans arrived in India they found the dark-skinned Dravidians. It was partly to separate the invaders from the vanquished that a system called "caste" became an important part of Hindu belief. The Aryans considered themselves superior to the Dravidians, and made rules which divided the two peoples.

It was from this division that the Hindu caste system gradually developed, until eventually all the people belonged to one of the hundreds of different castes many of which continue to this day. At the very top are the Brahmans (also sometimes spelled Brahmins) who are a priestly caste: in Hindu terms, they are thought to have come as near as humanly possible to perfection. In the course of history the Brahmans became very powerful.

Below the Brahmans there are many grades of caste; the people in the lowest caste (Sudra) are called Untouchables. An Untouchable must not be touched by a member of any other caste. He could not, until recent years, worship at a Hindu temple. He could not walk on a public road, and could only be employed in the lowliest and dirtiest jobs.

A member of one caste cannot "graduate" into a higher caste, and members of one caste may not marry or be friendly with members of another. Only death, according to Hindu belief, can change a man's caste. After death, a man may be reborn into a higher caste.

During the earlier centuries of Hindu rule, all the people of the Indian subcontinent shared these beliefs. It was not until the arrival of a wave of new invaders, beginning in the eighth century

Cattle and horses live very close to thatched village houses. In the center of this compound is a well, with water pots waiting to be filled.

A.D., that a new religion began to divide the Indian people. We shall read about this new religion later. For the moment, let's learn about a religion which developed from Hinduism and was to become important in both India and Pakistan.

Siddhartha Gautama, who became known as the Buddha, was a prince who was born in 563 B.C. He believed that man was evil but that purification came, not only through reincarnation, but by practicing good deeds and pure thoughts. Buddha did not divide people into castes. Although he was a Brahman and became a great and beloved teacher, he did not consider himself necessarily superior to people of lower caste. Many Indians became followers of Buddha, including the great Emperor Asoka. Helped by Asoka's interest, the religion of Buddha spread to many other lands. China, Korea, Japan, Cambodia, Burma, Thailand, and Sri Lanka are among the Asian nations which are largely Buddhist to

38

this day. And early in its history, Buddhism became a very important religion to the people living in the area we now know as Pakistan. We know this because of ruins which have been found.

The largest collection of ancient Buddhist remains in India or Pakistan are found at Taxila. Near Peshawar there is a small town called Takht Bahi which has the finest Buddhist buildings anywhere in the world.

It is strange that Buddhism has almost died out both in India and in Pakistan. Buddha is still considered a Hindu saint; but, for the most part, the people eventually went back to their Hindu beliefs, although the two religions influenced each other and borrowed from each other. In fact, Buddhism took firmest hold in lands outside India and it still flourishes in many of them. Buddha, who was a modest man, would hardly approve of the huge images in his likeness which are now worshiped in those

Farmers, taking a break from work, share a communal pipe.

countries, nor would he approve of the many superstitions now connected with Buddhism.

Of course, the forebears of modern Pakistanis and Indians shared in the development of the Hindu religion and culture, since there was no division between them before the new invaders' religion arrived. Modern Indians and Pakistanis are a mixture of the peoples who lived in the Indian subcontinent centuries ago, and of the many early Aryan invaders who came through the Khyber Pass.

But their history is long, and now we come to the period which divided the people of the Indian subcontinent into Indians and Pakistanis; for new invaders came, bringing a religion so different from Hinduism that the two had difficulty in existing together.

4

The Muslim Invaders

The prophet Mohammed was born in Mecca, on the Arabian peninsula, in 570 A.D. Mohammed received revelations from God, and these were written down and preserved in a book called the Koran. The religion established by Mohammed and named after him has become one of the most important in the world. We have mentioned already that believers in this religion are called Mohammedans, Moslems, or Muslims, and that the religion is also known as Islam.

Mohammed was a great prophet and followers flocked to his side. Within a few years of his death, there were tens of thousands of Muslims. By the year 732 A.D., just 100 years after Mohammed's death, fierce Muslim armies had conquered the whole of the Middle East and North Africa, and had even crossed into Spain. They threatened to engulf all Europe. Then, in 732, the Muslim armies were defeated near Poitiers in France. Had this not happened, all Europe might have become Muslim; and it is possible to imagine that both Europeans and Americans might today be followers of this religion. Certainly, the history of the world would have been very different.

For many years even the holy places of the Christian world were controlled by the great Muslim emperors or sultans. The crusades, for example, were fought by European Christians to free Jerusalem from Muslim domination.

Before we learn how the Muslims came to control Pakistan, let's learn about Muslim beliefs. A Muslim believes in one God, who is called Allah. Mohammed was his prophet, and the Koran is the Muslim bible in which Mohammed's revelations from God are preserved. The basic belief can be understood from this sentence from the Muslim creed: "There is no God but Allah, and Mohammed is his Prophet."

Muslims believe in a resurrection and a last judgement. They believe that if a man lives in accordance with the teachings of the Koran, he will attain an after-life in Paradise. The Muslim is democratic in his beliefs; for him, all men are created equal in the sight of God. Muslims reject the caste system, for it creates inequality. Muslims eat all meat except pork; this includes beef, the meat of the animal most sacred to Hindus. Above all, the Muslim has a fierce belief in *one* God, while the Hindu worships many gods.

Both Hinduism and Islam are ways of life which have influenced millions of people. Islam today is not only the religion of the Middle East, but of North Africa, Malaysia, and Indonesia. There are millions of Muslims in China also.

Now let's learn how this religion came to India, to produce, in time, two independent and different nations. In 712 A.D., one year after the Muslim armies entered Spain, the Arabs, under their 17-year-old leader General Mohammed Bin Qasim, penetrated into the heart of Sind, in what is now Pakistan. He routed the army of the Hindu king and, in 713 A.D., the whole of Sind and the Lower Punjab came under Muslim domination.

For over two centuries, the Muslims were content with these small areas. However, near the end of the 10th century other Muslim warriors began to descend upon India.

In 998 A.D., a king called Amir Sabuktigin crossed from Central Asia and raided Indian territory. With this raid began a series of invasions by Muslim rulers from Central Asia. The greatest of these invaders was Mahmud of Ghazni.

The Hindus fought bravely. They used war elephants, while the Muslims were mounted on fast horses. The elephants were powerful but slow. The mounted Muslim warriors could easily outdistance them.

The Hindus were also weakened by the caste system, for fighting was supposed to be the duty only of members of the warrior caste. Thousands of Hindus were massacred in the battles. Many Hindu temples were destroyed or looted.

Mahmud of Ghazni's men were content with hit-and-run raids. But in 1175 Mohammed Ghori, another Muslim warrior, came with his armies, not merely to loot, but to conquer and stay. By the year 1200, Mohammed Ghori controlled all of what is now Pakistan and much of northern India up to the gates of Delhi. When he died, one of his generals established headquarters at

Delhi, and it was from there that Muslim sultans ruled much of India until 1525. In that year another horde of invaders, also Muslims, poured through the Khyber Pass. Babur, chief of the new invaders, was a Muslim Turk, a descendant of both Genghis Khan and Tamerlane. Babur's army numbered only 12,000 men, but within two years he had defeated the armies of the Delhi sultans. Babur then founded the Mogul dynasty, the line of Muslim emperors in India.

The Mogul dynasty became the greatest in Indian history. Akbar, grandson of Babur, ascended the throne in 1556 when he was only 13 years old. The boy emperor defeated a strong Hindu army and became known as Akbar the Great.

Akbar was a man of great vision. Before his time, Muslim

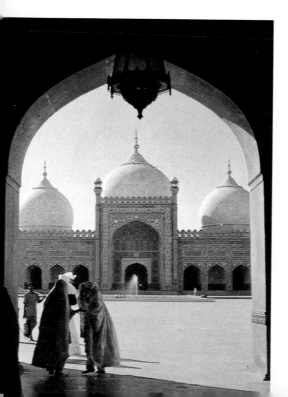

The beautiful Badshahi mosque at Lahore, built by the Mogul emperors.

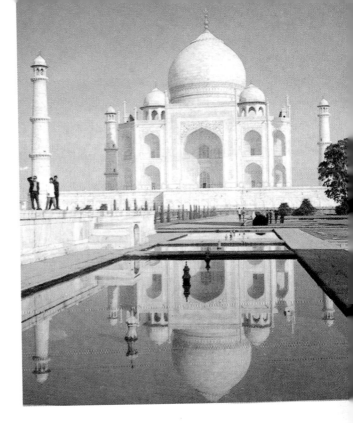

The Taj Mahal at Agra in India.

rulers had persecuted Hindus: all Hindus had to pay a special tax, and few Hindus could find employment in the government. Akbar changed all this, for he wanted all his subjects to live together in harmony. He wanted people to be united in common loyalty to their ruler and country. The tax imposed on Hindus was abolished, and they were even able to obtain jobs in the Mogul government. No longer were Hindu temples destroyed and looted.

By 1576, Akbar had become the ruler of the whole of India from the Himalayas down to the middle of the Indian peninsula.

His empire was probably the best organized and most efficiently ruled in the world. The empire was divided into a dozen provinces. A just and efficient tax system was established. A royal mint produced coins which were better designed than any in the world at that time. Akbar, who became known as the Grand Mogul, ruled at the time when Queen Elizabeth I was on the English throne. Historians believe that he was just as great and wise a ruler as England's famous queen. Unfortunately, the emperors who followed were neither wise nor tolerant. There were many intrigues within the Mogul court. People were heavily and unjustly taxed. The Shah Jehan, Akbar's grandson, began again to levy a special tax on Hindus, and they were often persecuted.

The Moguls were powerful and wealthy rulers and great builders. Shah Jehan was especially interested in architecture. He built the famous Taj Mahal at Agra in India. This beautiful monument was built in memory of his wife Mumtaz Mahal. Twenty thousand workers labored for 23 years to build the Taj Mahal which is often called the world's most beautiful building.

The last powerful Mogul emperor was Aurangzeb who ruled from 1658 to 1707. He was a very staunch Muslim. Having made his part of India into a purely Muslim state, he turned his attention to conquest. For nearly 10 years, the armies of Aurangzeb fought against the independent kingdoms of the subcontinent, until he finally conquered them.

Aurangzeb's empire extended from the Himalayas to Cape Comorin, India's most southerly point, and from the Ganges valley to the Indus valley. But the rule was harsh, and revolts broke out. For the last 15 years of his reign, Aurangzeb was busy leading his huge armies from one part of the country to another. He died, leading his troops, when he was 90 years old.

Although the Mogul court lasted for 150 years after Aurangzeb's death, the emperors had little power. As had so often happened in the past, India became divided into scores of small kingdoms. Some were ruled by Muslim kings, others by Hindu rajahs. There was frequent war and revolution; bandits swarmed through the land.

The Moguls were too weak and their land too divided to resist the new invaders who first arrived during the reign of Akbar's son, Jehangir. Before we learn about these newcomers, let's see what effect Muslim rule had on the people.

We have learned that there were periods when Muslims and Hindus lived peacefully together. At other times, the Muslim rulers persecuted the Hindus, destroyed their temples and imprisoned their priests. The most important effect of Muslim rule was that almost a quarter of the people became Mohammedans. This came about partly through intermarriage between Muslims and Hindus, and partly because some Hindus were forced to accept the new religion. For the most part, however, Hindus became Muslims voluntarily. Some did so in order to escape the tax on non-Muslims, others in order to get better jobs.

Two areas had the greatest proportion of Muslims. The Indus valley region, which we now know as Pakistan, had many Muslims because the invaders always arrived in this area first.

The lower valleys of the Ganges and Brahmaputra, a region known as Bengal, and now partly in Bangladesh, also had a high proportion of Muslims. This area was conquered by Muslims in 1202; but its ports had also often been visited by Arab ships.

The tomb of Jehangir, one of the last Mogul rulers.

Wherever they lived, Muslims differed from their neighbors mainly in religion. It has been said that fewer than 10 percent of Muslims are of "foreign" blood. By this we mean descendants of Arabs, Turks, Afghans, or Mogul conquerors.

During the centuries of Muslim rule, the two great religious groups borrowed some ideas from one another. Muslims believed in *purdah* for their women. This means that the women lived secluded lives, rarely going out. When they did leave their houses, their faces were heavily veiled. Numerous Hindu women accepted *purdah*. In some areas Hindu dietary laws were followed by Muslims. For instance, there are some Muslims who will not eat beef.

Muslim rule affected the Hindu religion too. In some areas, caste almost disappeared, and much of the power of the Brahmans was lost. Some Hindus began to question the caste system, to suggest change. One result of this was the establishment of a new, quite different sect known as the Sikhs.

Sikhs believe in one God and do not believe in caste. A Sikh man never cuts his hair, which is wound into a top-knot. The Sikh covers his head with a turban and always wears a beard.

During the centuries of Muslim rule there were also changes in material ways. The most important of these was in the matter of clothing. The Muslim conquerors came from areas where it was colder than in most of India, so that they had to dress warmly. In addition, they had learned to appreciate beautiful fabrics. We might say that the Hindus began to dress up under the Muslim influence.

A modern mosque in Karachi. The elaborate tower, which is called a minaret, contrasts rather oddly with the square lines of the building.

The Mogul emperors were great builders. We have mentioned the Taj Mahal, built by the Shah Jehan. Many other royal tombs and beautiful mosques were built during the Mogul rule. (A mosque is a Muslim church.)

We have learned that the language of the Aryan invaders was Sanskrit, and that many modern Indian languages developed from this ancient written language. The Moguls also influenced language when Urdu became the language of the Mogul court. Urdu is written in the Persian script and contains many Persian and Arabic words. Many people began to speak Urdu, or a mixture of Urdu and Hindi called Hindustani.

We have now seen something of how closely the histories of Pakistan and India are related. There were periods, lasting for

50

centuries, when the whole of the vast territory followed the Hindu way of life. There were other periods when the Muslims were in power and it was safer to follow Muslim ways.

Religion has always been important here. For some while Buddhism had many followers, and from time to time religious leaders founded new religions. But most people in the Indian subcontinent were either Hindus or Muslims. As we have said, when new invaders came in the 17th century, about one person in every four followed the teachings of Mohammed.

Now we will read about the newcomers, and the events which led to the establishment of the two free and independent nations

5

Spices Lead to British Rule

Plants, especially those which produce things we can eat or fibers which we use in making our clothes, have played an important part in the world's history.

The tea plant, discovered in the hills of southern China 1,700 years ago, traveled by ship and caravan to Europe. From Europe, tea went to the New World. Tea, because of the Boston Tea Party, helped to bring about the American Revolution.

Because of cotton and the great plantations which developed in the southern states of America, slavery became profitable. Slavery finally became the issue that started the American Civil War.

In Asia, pepper and other spices such as cloves, nutmeg, and cinnamon, changed the course of history. Because of spices, wars were fought; and nations changed their religion. Because of spices, Christopher Columbus and other explorers discovered the Western Hemisphere—they were looking for a short cut to India and the Spice Islands. And because of spices all of southern Asia and most of southeast Asia came under the rule of Europeans.

During the Middle Ages, there was much trade between India and the Ottoman Empire. This was a powerful Muslim empire which controlled most of the Middle East and had its capital in what is now Turkey. During this time the Muslim world and the Christian peoples of western Europe were bitter enemies. The spices of Asia reached Turkey but got no farther. So it was that Europeans had little with which to flavor their food.

In search of spices, Europe's sea captains defied the belief of most people at the time that the world was flat. They sailed on trips which sometimes lasted for years. And many of the explorers were lost at sea or in some strange or faraway land

A Portuguese named Vasco da Gama was the first European to reach India. His ships called at the port of Calicut on the southwest coast of India. They picked up a cargo of spices which excited not only the Portuguese. News of Vasco da Gama's cargo spread, and soon many ships were sailing around Africa or trying to reach the land of spices by sailing westward across the Atlantic.

The Portuguese were followed by the Dutch, the British, and the French. Each nation tried to establish trading posts, or factories as they were called. Partly because they were poor governors, the Portuguese began to lose ground. The Dutch gained control of the Molucca or Spice Islands (now part of Indonesia). This was one of the factors which caused the British to turn to the mainland of Asia, founding their factories on the coast of India.

Holland was a great seafaring nation in the 16th century and, as the Dutch were also good businessmen, they soon gained control of the Spice Islands and the pepper business. In England, meanwhile, in 1600, merchants had banded together to form the East India Company, hoping to take the spice trade from the Dutch or to develop their own factories. As we have said, the British, unable to push the Dutch from the Spice Islands, had turned to the mainland of Asia. They established trading posts at Bombay on India's west coast and at Madras and Calcutta on the east coast.

The East India Company was an unusual business concern. It had its own army and its own system of government; we might say that it was in partnership with the British government. But the company did not immediately gain control of India. It was not until the Mogul empire began to fall apart after the death of Aurangzeb that the company made much progress. And first it had to fight a series of battles with the Portuguese and the French.

After Aurangzeb's death, the British began to acquire great territory. Often they would make treaties with the many independent Muslim and Hindu rulers who came to power. The rulers would be allowed considerable authority and sometimes they were glad to have British protection. The British had to fight some wars against Indians too. The Gurkhas, a people living in Nepal,

In parts of the subcontinent elephants like this one are still commonly used for heavy work.

Growing rice in an irrigated area.

were subdued in 1818. They were forced to sign a treaty giving up certain districts in Bengal. Thereafter, they became great fight ers within the British army. The fierce and warlike Sikhs were defeated in 1849; and the British then became supreme over all India.

The British built a new city called New Delhi, alongside Delhi which was the Mogul capital, and this became the center of government. In time, the British government took over control from the East India Company, and India became Britain's largest and most important colony. Sir Winston Churchill once said that two out of every 10 people in England at one time received their income directly or indirectly from British business in the Indian subcontinent.

The Persian waterwheel—a primitive method of irrigation still used in Pakistan today. A circle of buckets dips into a well or a river and brings up water which is channeled to the fields.

We can understand how it was possible for Britain to conquer so many people when we remember that the population of India was divided in itself into Muslims and Hindus, and that the Hindus were further divided into castes. In addition, they were divided by the more than 800 dialects and 14 main languages which were spoken. India was large in area and in population but weak in unity and leadership.

During the 150 years of their domination of India (called "the British raj"), the British built roads and railways, and established a postal and telegraph system. They also built many schools and hospitals, and opened their own universities to Indian students. But, efficient though the British administration was, as with all colonial powers the country tended to be divided into the rulers and the ruled; and, as more and more Indians became educated, they began to long for their own independence.

The names of Mohandas Gandhi and Jawaharlal Nehru are well known to the world—these men were leaders in India's fight for independence. But few people can name a Pakistani who played a major part in this struggle. One reason for this is that the word "Pakistan" was unknown at that time—it was only coined as partition drew near. And, for a long period, the men most active in fighting for independence were Hindus. This is perhaps because, in the period after the Mogul empire became weak, the Muslims of India lost influence. They were much slower to learn about the new ways and progress brought by the British. Hindus took more quickly to new ideas, and became better businessmen. Muslim religious leaders urged their people to stay away from the new schools. And so, in business, education, medicine, and politics, the Muslims lagged behind.

Yet Pakistanis claim that the first real blow for freedom was indirectly struck by Muslims at the time of the Indian Mutiny, as far back as 1857. But while it may well have been the first blow, it also put the Muslim people under a cloud and possibly delayed independence for many years; for the Indian Mutiny, as we shall see, changed the thinking of many Englishmen about eventual freedom for their huge colony.

6

Independence and Partition

We have already learned how internal conflicts, war, and revolts had weakened and destroyed the unity of the country.

The effect of this disunity was to make it easy for foreign powers to conquer the country; when the British and French, who came initially as traders in the early 17th century, saw a country politically unstable, they immediately took advantage of the chaotic situation; and the British began steadily and successfully to establish their rule over the whole of the subcontinent.

Yet the Muslims were not to surrender without a struggle. In 1857, they made one final spurt to overthrow the British. This struggle is known in Pakistan's histories as the First War of Independence; in British history it is known as the Indian Mutiny.

Wherever the British ruled they recruited native soldiers to serve in their armed forces. This was also done in India, the locally recruited soldiers being called *sepoys*. As we might suppose, many sepoys were Muslims or Sikhs.

A Pakistani fisherman casting his net in an expert and traditional manner.

On May 10, 1857, the sepoys of an army unit in northern India were issued with cartridges coated with a protective grease, and a rumor spread that the grease had been made from pig fat. Most of the sepoys in this particular unit were Muslims. They refused to use the cartridges because Muslims believe that the pig is an unclean animal. As a result, a large number of Muslim troopers were placed under arrest and court-martialed.

Two days later, Muslim troops in Delhi, the old Mogul capital, revolted and pledged their allegiance to the Mogul Emperor Bahadur Shah Zafar. (We have read that the Mogul court still existed although it had very little power.)

The uprising which began on May 10, 1857, lasted until April 1858. Most of the fighting was confined to northern India. Many battles were fought with great ferocity, bitterness, and cruelty.

59

This British-built clock tower is a reminder of the long years of British rule.

The Muslims fought fiercely but failed in their bid to overthrow the British, who were often aided by provincial dynasties.

They were finally defeated and crushed, and the last Mogul emperor and his family were banished from India.

The British victory was a fatal blow to Muslim power in the subcontinent. The sun now began to set over a people who had ruled India for 800 years. The breakup of the Mogul empire was at hand. The Moguls had not only lost their political power; in addition, they were stripped of all prestige and dignity. As a nation, they slipped into a state of political indifference and backwardness.

Because of the war, the Muslim community resisted western ideas for many years. This fact, combined with the effect of the uprising, made them take a back seat in Indian affairs. Efforts to make changes, and to take a greater part in government affairs, were therefore largely left to the Hindus. There were, however, some Muslims who began to play an important role. One of these was Sir Syed Ahmad Khan. In 1869 Syed Ahmad Khan visited England and Europe and was much impressed by the progress of European people. When he returned home, he began to tell his people that they must lay aside superstition and age-old ways. He reminded Muslims that Mohammed, their prophet, had said: "Go even to the walls of China for the sake of learning."

Sir Syed (he was knighted by Queen Victoria) founded the famous Aligarh Muslim University. He worked for better relations between Muslims and Hindus. He began to stir his people, and to encourage more and more Muslims to become educated.

However, in spite of Sir Syed's efforts, the leadership in the freedom movement continued for many years to be Hindu. Just before the First World War, Mohandas Gandhi returned to India from South Africa. Gandhi had been educated in England and had gone to South Africa to practice law. While there, he had fought for better working conditions for Indians living in that country. He led the Indians in South Africa in peaceful demonstrations of passive resistance to domination, in sit-down strikes, and in what was to become known as "civil disobedience."

Gandhi's methods were very successful in South Africa, and he became a hero when he returned to India. For years he led India's struggle for independence, using the same methods of civil disobedience, of fasting, and of nationwide strikes which stopped business activities. Gandhi and Nehru became the leaders of the National Congress Party of India, which later became the most powerful political party in the country.

The First World War also created more agitation for freedom among Muslims. During this war, Great Britain fought against Turkey, which was allied with Germany. Turkey was then head of

A street typical of both India and Pakistan.

what was known as the Ottoman Empire. Its ruler was called the caliph, and was considered by all Muslims to be the elected head of the Muslim peoples. Istanbul, capital of the Ottoman Empire, was also the center of the Muslim world, just as Rome is considered the center of the Catholic world.

When the Western Allies won the war, all the territories in the Middle East which had been part of the Ottoman Empire were taken away. Muslims everywhere considered the peace terms much too severe. In protest they began what was called the Khilafat Movement. Muslims in India protested to the British against the severe peace terms. Like the Hindus of the Congress Party, they also decided to try non-violent methods of protest. Although the Khilafat Movement did not change the terms of the peace treaty with Turkey, it did serve to unite Muslims against British rule in India.

During these years of struggle, Muslims and Hindus often worked together in India. Numerous prominent Muslims became members of the National Congress Party. Other Muslims worked only through their own organization, which was formed in 1906 and was called the All-India Muslim League. At first, leaders, whether Muslim or Hindu, thought only in terms of freedom for the whole of India. They did not talk about separate nationhood for Muslims and Hindus.

It was Dr. Mohammed Iqbal, a great poet and philosopher, who first suggested an independent Muslim state. Later, Iqbal was joined in this idea by the man whom Pakistanis consider the founder of their nation. His name was Mohammed Ali Jinnah, and he came to be called the *Quaid-i-Azam*, which means "Great Leader."

Jinnah was born in 1876 in Karachi. He completed his school studies at the age of 15. Then he went to England to study law, returning to India in 1896 after completing his education. In 1909, at the age of 33, he was elected to the Imperial Legislative Council, and at first he worked unceasingly for Hindu-Muslim unity and constitutional reforms.

Jinnah was a member of the Hindu-dominated Congress Party. But he resigned from it in 1920 when he realized that the policies of the Congress Party were not beneficial to Muslims. Thereafter, he devoted himself entirely to defending and safeguarding Muslim rights.

Jinnah sincerely believed that the future of the Muslims under a Hindu majority rule was dark; he feared that they would always be dominated and that their rights would not be upheld. In 1930, Jinnah decided that there could never be unity and peace between the two great religions. The only hope for the Muslims lay in having a separate homeland of their own, a homeland where they could live according to their own culture and religion, and rule themselves as they had done in the past.

To understand Ali Jinnah's attitude we must understand how bitterness began to grow between the two religious groups. It may seem strange to us, but cows were often the cause of trouble. As we have learned, while the cow is sacred to Hindus, Muslims like beef. Sometimes Muslims would deliberately offend Hindus by making a great to-do over the slaughtering of a cow. Hindus

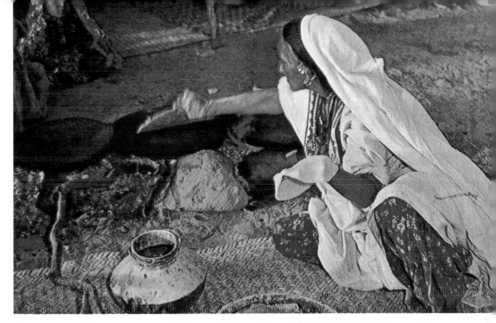

Cooking chapatties—one of the traditional foods of both Pakistan and India.

would retaliate by holding noisy festivals and religious ceremonies at the very time when Muslims were worshiping.

Often serious riots broke out between Muslims and Hindus and hundreds of people were killed. Sometimes these riots occurred because Hindus staged noisy processions near mosques. Year after year, the tension between Muslims and Hindus increased. On several occasions, Muslims refused to join in the civil disobedience campaigns started by Gandhi. When Muslim shop-owners refused to close their stores, they were attacked by Hindu mobs.

Meanwhile, the British government had been forced into giving India greater independence, a greater voice in its own government. One of the British concessions was to give the provinces self-government. Members of the provincial legislatures were elected by the people.

A farm in Pakistan.

Unfortunately, the Congress Party, which had become very powerful, took advantage of these reforms. Muslims became alarmed because the Congress Party was able to control so many elections. In addition, the provincial governments, dominated by the Congress Party, attempted to enforce Hindi as the official language.

Gradually, it became clear that if Britain gave India freedom, there must be two new nations based upon religion. In 1933, the name *Pakistan* was first suggested. As we have said, this means "Land of the Pure." But the name was not chosen only for its meaning; rather it came from the initials of some provinces of northwest India which Muslim leaders wanted to be within an independent Muslim state. Thus the "P" stands for Punjab; the "K" for Kashmir; the "S" for Sind, etc.

In the years just before and during the Second World War, the demand for independence increased. The British government offered many different plans which Hindu leaders, Muslim leaders, or sometimes leaders of both groups, would not accept. Finally, in the middle of the war, the British offered complete independence. The only condition was that first the war must be won. As soon as the war was over, British soldiers would leave, and India would be free.

Neither Congress Party nor Muslim League leaders would accept this offer because they felt that winning the war was not relevant. Some of the Hindu leaders, especially Gandhi, turned bitterly against the British.

However, when the Allies finally did win the war, the British kept their promise. Independence and freedom came to India at midnight, August 14, 1947.

Before the British parliament granted independence, there were more riots between Hindus and Muslims. There were now many serious problems to be worked out. If freedom was to be granted on the basis of religion, the two parts of the new Pakistan would be separated by a vast stretch of Indian territory. We have already read that the greatest concentrations of Muslims were to be found in the Indus valley in the west and the lower Ganges valley in the east.

There were also many difficult problems in connection with the small princely states. Some of these states were ruled by Hindu rajahs but had Muslim populations; in other states, ruled by Muslims, most of the people were Hindus. For instance, Hyderabad in Central India had a population of 30,000,000. For centuries this rich state had been ruled by Muslims, but most of the population was Hindu. Should Hyderabad be a part of India or a part of the new Pakistan? Indian leaders claimed that Hyderabad should join the new India. However, this state had been a center of Muslim culture for many years. Muslim leaders naturally wanted it to become a part of their new nation.

On the other hand, the rich state of Kashmir was ruled by Hindu maharajahs, but 85 percent of its people were Muslims. To make matters more difficult, there was no part of the subcontinent in which all the people were either Muslim or Hindu. There were some Hindus and some Muslims living in every region. If the new nations were to be established entirely on the basis of religion, tens of millions of Muslims and Hindus would have to move and find new houses.

These were some of the problems which faced Mohammed Ali Jinnah (who became the first Governor-General of Pakistan) and the Indian leaders when the two new nations came into existence at midnight on August 14, 1947. As a result, within a few days, Hindus, Muslims, and Sikhs began to murder one another.

These Pakistani farmers are celebrating the completion of a road built with American help. The earliest roads in the country were built by the British.

Hundreds of villages were burned down; thousands of women and children were kidnaped or murdered. People were butchered simply because of their religion. Hundreds of thousands began to flee for their lives. Hindus who found themselves living in a Muslim state tried to get to Hindu territory. Nearly 7,000,000 Muslims escaped into Pakistan territory.

The killing continued through August, September, and October of 1947. It might have ended in war, had not Gandhi started his last fast in order to force Indian leaders to stop the campaign against Muslims. Gandhi's fast helped to bring the people, already shocked by the killings, to their senses. But, on January 30, 1948, a Hindu fanatic, who wanted all Muslims to be killed, assassinated Gandhi.

Hindus and Muslims alike were horrified by the death of Gandhi. Through his civil disobedience campaigns and his fasts, he was in many ways responsible for the freedom which had at last come for Muslims and Hindus alike. He had become a world-famous figure. For 30 years his life had shaped the history of India. In death he made his greatest contribution by causing people to come to their senses. Disagreements still existed, but at least they were faced without bloodshed—or rather without much bloodshed—until 1971.

Now let's learn about the newly created Pakistan, its many problems and its people. Certainly, few nations have become independent in worse circumstances, or paid a heavier price in blood and misery.

7

Divided Pakistan

Both India and Pakistan faced many unusual problems when they became free and independent nations in 1947. However, the problems of the new Muslim nation of Pakistan were even more difficult than those faced by India.

Pakistan was divided into an eastern section and a western section, with more than 1,000 miles (more than 1,600 kilometers) of India between them. The peoples of the two sections had little in common, except the Muslim religion, and were inclined to distrust each other. Their country had no capital and no government buildings. New Delhi, the capital of British India for many years, was now Indian. The large government buildings, and all the files and records of government, were in that city.

The postal system, the telegraph lines, the roads, railways, dams and irrigation canals had been planned for one huge country.

The status of Kashmir, the Hindu-ruled Muslim state to the north of West Pakistan, had not yet been settled. While millions of Muslims had fled from their homes into East and West

The Empress Market in Karachi. The former capital was built by the British.

Pakistan, many more millions still remained in India. Equally well, over 10 million Hindus found themselves living in Pakistan. Many people could not afford to flee; others were unwilling to leave villages in which their families had lived for generations.

East Pakistan, while smaller in area, had a larger population than West Pakistan. When Karachi, in West Pakistan, was selected as the national capital, East Pakistanis were angry and apprehensive. After all, there were more people in East Pakistan. Why should the capital be far away in the West?

Karachi was a seaport with 400,000 people, but the population soon grew to over a million. Into this city without government buildings came thousands of clerks and officials. For months, tents were used instead of offices, and these were often without desks, telephones, or electricity. Often, important government records were lost or had been left in New Delhi. In addition, tens of thousands of refugees swelled the population of the new capital; they had nowhere to live, and had to be cared for and fed.

There were differences of opinion among the Pakistani leaders as to what kind of government should be developed. Some devoutly religious men wanted to have a strictly Muslim state, with the beliefs of their religion imposed upon all citizens. There were also leaders who wanted Urdu, the principal language of West Pakistan, to be the language of all Pakistan. Naturally, the Bengali-speaking people of East Pakistan did not like this. The East Pakistanis became fearful that, with the government far away in Karachi, they would always be "poor relations" to the West Pakistanis.

Furthermore, for some years after the creation of Pakistan in 1947, no national elections had been held. Politicians were ruining the country by corrupt and inefficient practices. They had little interest in the affairs of the nation. To make matters worse, only one out of every eight Pakistanis could read or write. Economic and social conditions began to deteriorate. High prices, shortage of food and the high cost of living created bitter feelings in the rural areas. In East Pakistan the members of the assembly had beaten the Speaker and later killed his deputy. In West Pakistan, the chief minister had been murdered.

These disturbing conditions aroused fears that Pakistan was on the verge of collapse. Urgent steps were necessary if the nation was to be saved from utter disaster. To save the country from further ruin, General Ayub Khan, the commander-in-chief of the army, took over the government of the country on October 7, 1958. It was one of the most peaceful and bloodless army revolutions in history.

On taking over, the new regime began immediately to root out corruption and malpractice. The capital was moved from Karachi to Rawalpindi, partly so that the government could not be said to be influenced by business interests. The previously forgotten homeless refugees were resettled in new houses especially constructed for them. Massive industrial and agricultural programs were launched to develop the country and raise the standard of living of the people. The parliamentary government, which until that time had been modeled on the British system, was changed to a presidential form of government with the president as the chief executive.

The president was assisted by a Cabinet of Ministers who, as in the United States, were appointed by the president and were not members of the legislature.

The National Assembly consisted of 156 members, divided equally between representatives of East and West Pakistan. Of these, six had to be women. In addition to the National Assembly, East and West Pakistan each had its own elected assembly.

In the early part of 1965, national elections were held for the first time in 17 years and Field Marshal Ayub Khan was re-elected president for another five-year term.

Further evidence of Pakistan's progress was provided by the fact that, although it proclaimed itself an Islamic republic, there was freedom of worship in the country for all people. The only position which had to be filled by a Muslim was that of the president. Other offices were open to all citizens regardless of race, color or religious belief.

After Pakistan gained its independence, there were other difficulties to be overcome, besides those connected with the establishment of a strong government. We have mentioned some of these: the fact that so many people were illiterate, for example, and that several million refugees had to be fed and housed. Food shortage was one outstanding question when Pakistan became independent, and it is still difficult to produce enough food for the

A village in Pakistan. Note how parched and arid the land looks.

The Tarbela Dam on the Indus River—the world's longest rock-and-earth-filled dam.

large population. Also, in one way or another, water is a constant problem.

This brings us to the problem of Kashmir, which has created much tension between Pakistan and India. A huge irrigation system waters over 33 million acres (13 million hectares) of land in Pakistan. The water for Pakistan comes from rivers whose upper reaches are in Kashmir. That is why Kashmir is so necessary to the existence of Pakistan.

We read earlier that over 85 percent of the people of Kashmir are Muslims but, at the time of independence, they were ruled by a Hindu maharajah. This is another reason why Pakistan wanted to control Kashmir.

How then did India come to control a Muslim state? The inten-

Muslim herdsmen from the hills of Kashmir.

tion behind the agreements which led to partition was that the independent states would join India or Pakistan on the basis of the predominant religion of the local inhabitants. Areas where most people were Hindus would become part of India; states where most of the population were Muslims would become a part of Pakistan.

A few months after independence, Muslim tribesmen in Kashmir revolted against the maharajah. They feared that their ruler was going to join Kashmir to India in order to save his own position. The Sikh soldiers of the maharajah's army put down the revolt; whereupon many Muslim tribesmen from other areas invaded Kashmir. The invading tribesmen defeated the maharajah's army and pushed forward until they were close to Srinagar, the capital.

The maharajah then asked India for help. The Indian government sent troops by air, and they pushed back the Muslim soldiers and saved the capital for the maharajah. For several months

76

after that, it appeared that there might be war between India and Pakistan over Kashmir. India appealed to the United Nations, accusing Pakistan of aggression because it was helping the Muslim tribesmen who continued to fight India's troops.

The United Nations arranged for a cease-fire in Kashmir. They then recommended a plebiscite, which meant that the Kashmir people would put the matter to a vote and so decide for themselves whether to join India or Pakistan. Pakistan agreed to accept the results of a plebiscite; India also agreed, but never put the plebiscite into operation.

Indian soldiers have remained in eastern Kashmir, and the state is now claimed by India. Official Indian maps show it as a part of India. It is interesting to note that government of Pakistan maps show Kashmir and the smaller state of Jammu as "disputed territory."

There have been many other problems between India and Pakistan, including arguments over the borders between the two countries. Occasionally, Pakistani and Indian soldiers have engaged in border fights; and, in 1971, it seemed that some shooting across the border between India and Pakistan might lead to a full-scale war between the two countries.

The cause of the shooting was a very serious quarrel between the two sections of Pakistan. East and West had still failed to settle their differences. Not satisfied with their own East Pakistan assembly and an equal share of representatives in the National Assembly, many easterners wanted to govern themselves entirely. They supported a political party called the Awami League, led by

Sheikh Mujib ur Rahman. The Awami League won most of the seats in the assembly at an election in December 1970, and planned to bring in a new constitution which would give East Pakistan complete control over all its own affairs.

By this time, President Ayub Khan had resigned, after riots and violent demonstrations which the government could not control. His place had been taken by President Yahya Khan, another westerner. President Yahya Khan tried to block the Awami League by delaying a meeting of the Assembly. That led to more riots, as well as strikes and demonstrations throughout Pakistan. Fearing an armed rebellion, the president then declared martial law, and ordered the army to put down the disturbances. Sheikh Mujib was imprisoned, but his followers resisted the army. They declared that East Pakistan was now an independent state, with the name Bangladesh. And in a brief but bitter and very destructive war they forced the government to let them have their own way. The old West Pakistan was now the only Pakistan.

During the war, about eight million East Pakistanis who had lost their homes or felt in danger of losing them took refuge over the border, in India. Pakistan believed that India was arming some of these refugees, and helping them to make guerilla warfare on the government army. That caused the border shooting which for a time seemed likely to bring India into the war on the side of Sheikh Mujib's followers. It has also caused further suspicion and dissension between India and Pakistan since the war ended, especially as India has remained on friendly terms with Bangladesh.

In 1977 when riots following an election were violent, the army took over the government and put General Zia-ul-Haq in charge. General Zia was eventually declared president and he ruled through a council of mainly civilian advisors. Zia ruled Pakistan until he was killed in a plane crash in 1988. He made numerous reforms while in office but Pakistan continued to struggle. After his death Benazir Bhutto was elected prime minister, the first woman to head a modern Muslim country.

In 1990 Bhutto's government was accused of corruption. Her successor Mian Sharif was in turn accused of corruption in 1993. Facing a crippled economy Bhutto was then reelected prime minister.

Then in 1996 she was dismissed from office by President Farooq Leghari again under charges of corruption and mismanagement. A new election was held in 1997 and Sharif was again elected with a large majority of the vote. Sharif now led a country in great need of economic reforms and aid.

If Pakistan is to play its full part as one of the largest Muslim nations in the world, it must have better relations with its neighbors. India and Pakistan working together could solve their problems and could give their nations a more important voice in world affairs. But tensions remain high between them and Pakistan has been accused of violating international arms agreements by testing nuclear weapons.

8

Living in Pakistan

Now let's learn about life in modern Pakistan. How do people live in the cities and in the country? What food is eaten, and what clothes are worn?

   If you were a boy living in Pakistan, your first name might be

Boys at school in Pakistan.

Mohammed, sometimes spelled Muhammed. This is one of the most common boy's names among Muslims. Indeed, wherever there are Muslims, whether it be in the Middle East or Indonesia, there are boys named Mohammed. Other common names are Ali, Ahmed, Amin and Husain (spelled Hussein in the Middle East).

Because they are Muslims, Mohammed, his friends, and their families would pray five times each day. As they pray, they would bow in the direction of Mecca. This is the city in Saudi Arabia where Mohammed the Prophet is buried. Mecca is holy to all Muslims; no matter where they may be or what they may be doing, the faithful turn toward Mecca in prayer five times a day.

The call to prayer is given from a minaret or tower which is often part of a mosque. Mohammed, his friends and their families would often go to the mosque to hear the word of God as read from the Koran. They would celebrate Ramadan, a religious festival: for a month, they would be fasting from sunrise to sunset each day.

There are several sects or denominations among Muslims. Mohammed and his friends might belong to different sects, but their main beliefs would be the same. As good Muslims they would hope some day to visit Mecca, the Holy City. It is the hope of all devout Muslims, wherever they may live, to go on this pilgrimage. However, most Pakistanis never manage to do so. You can see from the picture of a typical house that the standard of living is still fairly low and, although a pilgrim can visit Mecca very cheaply, the cost is more than many people can afford.

Apart from the standard of living, climate has much to do with

A village scene—houses are small and crowded and much of the life is carried on in the open air.

the construction of houses in Pakistan. If he lived in a rural area, Mohammed's house would be made of hardened clay or mud bricks. It might have a thatched roof, but a flat tile or mud roof would be more likely. These houses are small, often rectangular in shape. They have very little furniture. Mohammed and his brothers and sisters might have to sleep on the floor.

We know that Pakistan has a hot, dry climate, which is unsuitable for growing some of the more common crops of Asia. Mohammed and his family like rice. However, this food can only be served on very special occasions. Wheat, which is grown in the irrigated fields of the Punjab, is Pakistan's most important source of food.

Wheat is used in various ways. Mohammed's mother will often make *chapatties*, which are thin, unleavened pancakes. With the chapatties there will be meat and vegetables, often cooked with curry powder.

Curry is a very popular hot spice flavoring in Pakistan and India, and curried vegetables and meat are common dishes. We

82

know that good Muslims may not eat pork. Mohammed's family, therefore, do not eat pork at all; of the meat available to them they like mutton more than beef. Some Pakistanis have an idea that beef is hard to digest. However, it is often eaten because it is less expensive than mutton.

Mohammed's mother may also make *kebab*. This is barbecued mutton, cooked with many spices; it is very good. Whatever the meal may be, Mohammed and his family will eat with their fingers. There are no knives and forks, nor do they use chopsticks

Oxen thresh wheat by trampling it underfoot.

as in China or Japan. Eating with one's fingers is not as messy as you may think. The chapatties are used to pick up and hold bits of meat and vegetables, so that a sort of bite-sized sandwich is made which is popped into the mouth.

Our illustrations include several pictures which show the kind of clothing worn in Pakistan. Pakistani clothing is loose-fitting, often white. Sometimes the men and boys wear shorts, but the baggy, pajama-like trousers, called a *shalwar*, are more common. A shirt is worn with these loose trousers and, if a man is dressed for a special occasion, a long high-collared coat, called a *sherwani*, is worn. You may have noticed too that in almost all the pictures the men are wearing turbans. Turbans are often wound around a skull cap called a *kulla*.

If Mohammed lives in the Punjab, he will tie his turban differently from the way it is tied in other parts of Pakistan. In fact, it is almost always possible to know what area a man is from by the way in which his turban is tied.

Mohammed's mother will probably wear a *shalwar* too. And with it she will wear a shirt called a *kamiz*, and a shawl called a

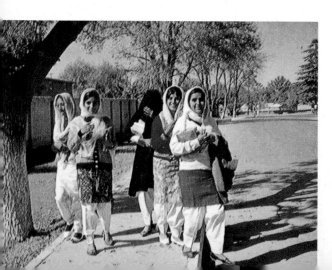

Pakistani schoolgirls.
Note that one is heavily
veiled.

duputta which covers the shoulders and goes over the head. For special occasions, a beautiful *sari* may be worn. This is a long length of silk or cotton, always in a lovely color, which is wound around the waist, and then drawn up around the shoulders or over the head. Women in Pakistan also often wear a kind of divided skirt called a *gharara*.

We have used the word purdah elsewhere in this book. Perhaps Mohammed's mother may live in *purdah*. This means that if guests come she stays in the kitchen, or in her own room if the house is large enough for her to have one. When she goes to market, or out in the street for any reason, she covers her face with her *duputta*. Traditional Muslims believe that a woman's place is at home, that she should be very modest, and that she should always cover her face in the presence of any men except those of her family.

However, times are changing in Pakistan. If Mohammed has an older sister, she may go to school, and she probably does not live in purdah. Pakistani girls are learning to be nurses, doctors, even flight attendants.

We can get some idea of how much things are changing in modern Pakistan from the numbers of children, both boys and girls, who now go to school. Mohammed's father and mother probably never went to school at all, and can neither read nor write. Illiteracy is one of Pakistan's greatest problems; but everywhere there are new schools being built, and soon schooling will become compulsory for all children.

In school, Mohammed would study many of the subjects studied in European schools. There would be history, geography, and arithmetic. The major difference between Mohammed's school and those in other countries is in the languages which must be studied. If Mohammed lives in the Punjab he will speak Punjabi, and his written language will probably be Urdu. However, if he lives in Sind, which is south of the Punjab, he will speak Sindhi, and his written language will also be Urdu. Wherever he lives in Pakistan, he will begin school in Urdu, because Urdu is the national language of Pakistan, and is used in schools.

From our picture we can see how Mohammed might write the Urdu alphabet. There are 38 letters or sounds in this way of writing. Instead of beginning on the left-hand side of the page as we do in English, Mohammed will begin on the right. As we have said, Urdu is written in Persian script and can also be read by the people of Persia—or Iran as we now call that country.

A caravan of Bactrian or mountain camels.

Because of the many curves and squiggles, it is difficult to write Urdu properly with a modern pen. Mohammed will use a pen or stylus made from a special kind of reed which grows in swampy places along the Indus River. After he has learned to write the flowing Urdu letters, he will discover that in his language there is a sort of shorthand. When letters are put together to form words, they are often shortened. Some of the dots and squiggles are left out.

After learning Urdu, Mohammed must also study English, which is the second language in Pakistan. In some secondary schools and colleges, English is used in teaching almost all subjects.

The English language is very important in Pakistan: it is the language of business, many newspapers and magazines are published in English, and many Pakistanis can speak to one another only in English because their own languages are so different. Of

A camel cart in the middle of one of Pakistan's largest cities.

course, now that everyone also studies Urdu, this language will soon become a means of communication for all the people in Pakistan, and it is expected that English will become less important as time goes by.

Since Pakistan is a poor country, Mohammed will have to walk to school. There are very few school buses, but there are many fine roads through the generally flat countryside. And there are some ordinary buses and trains. However, Mohammed and his family, being average folk, would probably travel to market or visit friends in a bullock cart, or *tonga*.

Notice the camels in our picture. Camels pull carts in Pakistan, and are sometimes used for plowing or for turning the wheels of flour mills. There are two kinds of camels. One has short hair. The other is shaggy and is called the bactrian, or mountain, camel. Oxen are even more important than camels as beasts of burden; oxcarts are used in many sections of Pakistan. The dung from oxen and camels is used for fuel in most homes, since there are few trees and most people cannot afford to buy wood or coal.

The Shalimar Gardens, Lahore.

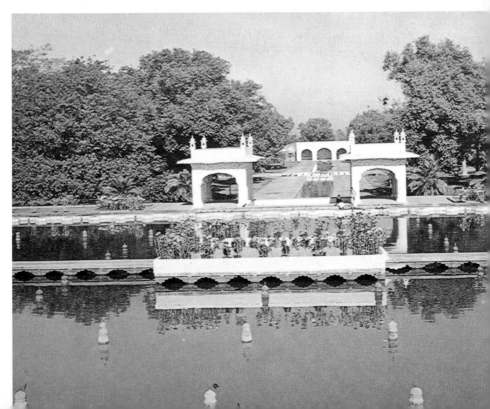

Fortunately, because the climate is hot except in the mountains, a fire is necessary only for cooking.

If Mohammed's family is typical, they will live in the country or in a small village. About 50 percent of the Pakistani people live by farming. But there are some large cities in Pakistan. Karachi, the former capital now has a population of close to 10 million. It is a city of wide streets and many new buildings. Even here, though, there are many camel carts. The camels often wear bells on their knees and flowers in their harnesses.

In the picture of the marketplace you can see the different methods of transportation used in Karachi. Near the clock tower

A marketplace in Karachi in the mid-1900s which shows clearly the contrast between ancient and modern, both in the surrounding buildings and in the various types of vehicles.

there are taxis and buses. Near the center of the picture there is a camel cart and a horse-drawn carriage called a *gharry*. In the foreground there are several pedicabs or rickshaws. A bicycle is used to pull this almost-square, two-wheeled vehicle.

Karachi lies northwest of the mouth of the Indus River. It is the largest city in Pakistan, and is famous for its natural harbor and its international airport. Ships from Europe, America, and the Far East call at Karachi. Its airport is busy, with modern jet airliners landing and taking off day and night, bringing Karachi within a few hours' of most of the capitals of the world. Because it was once the capital, Karachi became the nerve center of the business, commercial and industrial world; and though the importance of Karachi has since diminished, it still continues to conduct the country's big business.

Rawalpindi, another big city, is situated in the northern part of Punjab, near the famous snowcapped hills of Murree. It replaced Karachi as the temporary capital until the new capital, Islamabad, was completed in 1967. Islamabad, which took six years to build, stands on the dark brown Potwar Plateau not far from Rawalpindi. It is still a very small city but it is one of the most modern capitals in Asia.

Now we come to Lahore, the second largest city in Pakistan. It has a population of well over 2,500,000. Lahore is 811 miles (about 1,300 kilometers) away from Karachi and is an important religious and educational center.

This city was a favorite of the Mogul emperors. They planned some of the loveliest gardens and built some of the country's most

A view of modern Lahore, a city of wide traffic-filled streets and impressive buildings as well as some of the country's most famous ancient mosques and mausoleums.

famous mosques and mausoleums there. The beautiful Shalimar Gardens with their pools and fountains, and the mausoleum of Emperor Jehangir, still attract innumerable tourists. The Mogul emperors also built the world's largest mosque, called Badshahi, which is a most impressive sight with its many high arches and huge marble domes.

From Lahore we cross the country to Peshawar. Here the people are mainly Pathans, a brave and warlike people who have lived near the Khyber Pass for centuries.

These people, who live among the mountains of Pakistan, are different from those of the desert and the plains. In the mountains, there are many herdsmen; the job of a mountain boy may be to care for the sheep and goats. More clothing must be worn in the mountains, for there is often frost and snow. Yet in some of the mountain valleys rice can be grown, because they are sheltered from the cold and have a much higher rainfall than the rest of Pakistan.

The mountains are among the highest and roughest in the world, and so bring many foreign mountaineers to Pakistan. The Pakistanis themselves have not yet produced a great climber, but they do love games and are good athletes. The most popular games are cricket, hockey, squash, and soccer. Pakistan's hockey teams have won Olympic medals. And their cricket team has been known to beat England in test matches.

Pakistanis love to fly kites. They have interesting kite-flying contests. The kite strings are covered with glue and ground glass.

A water carrier—a familiar scene in Pakistan where many areas are never far from drought.

Each boy tries to force his kite string against those of other boys in such a way that the strings will be cut by the glass.

Perhaps it is kite-flying which makes many Pakistanis interested in aircraft. There is never a shortage of good pilots and aircraft technicians in Pakistan, and aircraft are used more and more to carry passengers and goods over the long distances within the country. The government also operates a fine airline called Pakistan International Airlines (PIA), whose big jets may be seen at most of the world's airports.

Pakistan Develops

Supplying food for a large and growing population is Pakistan's most urgent problem. Even though eight out of 10 Pakistanis live by farming, their work does not produce enough food to go around. So Pakistan, with all its farmland must import vast quantities of food each year to keep its population from hunger.

One reason for this is the nature of the country. With a low average rainfall in the best of years, much of the farmland is never very far from drought—and drought, of course, means poor crops or sometimes no crops at all. On the other hand, farmers in the long, low-lying river valleys are often troubled by too much water. When there are heavy rains or sudden thaws of snow in the mountains to the north, the rivers come down in flood, washing crops and topsoil away, and leaving fields waterlogged. Also, much farmland in the river valleys is spoiled because the very hot sun causes quick evaporation. This takes the necessary moisture from the soil, but leaves deposits of salt in which crops cannot grow.

Mechanical handling and transportation aids often contrast with traditional dress, as is shown here.

Also many Pakistani farmers do not grow food crops. They grow cotton to supply the weaving mills which keep many town-dwelling Pakistanis in employment, and to meet export orders from other countries, which make cotton goods but do not grow the raw material. Developing countries need town industries and the money that can be earned from exports, so Pakistan cannot do without its cotton crops.

Yet another reason for the food problem is the way in which the land is shared and treated—or rather the way in which it *was* shared and treated. Until recently, a great deal of the land was held by a fairly small number of rich people. They could stay rich without trying to make their land more productive, and so they left large areas idle or unimproved while many other people could not find enough farmland to keep them at work for more than

96

one-third of the year. Some farmers had to make do with less than one acre (about one-half hectare), and even in the well-watered Five Rivers area a Pakistani farmer needs at least 12.5 acres (about five hectares) to make a living.

However, there have been some big changes since West Pakistan became the only Pakistan. At that time, many West Pakistanis were nearly as discontented with their government and their standard of living as the East Pakistanis who had rebelled. Also, the country had lost a market as well as an important source of income and supplies when the rebellion won independence for the easterners. So when democratic government was restored, in 1972, its first task was to help the farming people and to make the farmland more productive.

About 1,000,000 acres (405,000 hectares) of land were taken from those who had too much and given to farmers who had too

Improved social conditions in Pakistan include medical services and hospitals such as the one in which this photograph was taken.

With other changes, Pakistan is introducing better training facilities for doctors. This is a medical college for women in Lahore.

little, or to landless people who wished to become farmers. Farmers who had been too poor to buy fertilizers, pest-killers, machinery, and better types of seed could have them, and were taught to use them. Irrigation was extended. Land made useless by erosion or by salt deposits was reclaimed. Better roads, more comfortable houses, and new markets were provided. Social welfare services for farmers' families were begun. And the results have improved the agricultural output and the lives of the people.

In all this rural improvement, the Pakistanis had much good advice and practical help from the United Nations. They also were helped by individual nations, particularly the United States and Britain.

In the modern world, no nation can be strong without factory industries, and while its farmers are learning to grow more food, Pakistan is also developing these industries. Indeed, it has been able to develop them more quickly and more successfully than it has developed its farmland. When it was part of British India, the whole country had only 34 factories. Most were very small, and apart from the cotton mills they produced mainly for the home market. But the factories of Pakistan increased. Many compete in the world markets with such exports as cloth, cement, and sporting goods, while others produce a wide range of goods for local use. These include sugar and other foods, fertilizers, bicycles, sewing machines, tools, paint, paper, and chemicals. There are also steel foundries, oil refineries, and a very busy shipbuilding yard.

Many of these industries were begun and developed under three "five-year plans" which spread over the years from 1955 to 1970, but they suffered a severe setback during the time when East Pakistan was struggling to become Bangladesh. Even when peace and democratic government were restored some industries were slow to pick up, and in 1972 the government took control of those on which other industries depended. Steel production, motor vehicle assembly, oil refining, heavy engineering and the manufacture of fertilizers and other important chemicals all became national industries.

After that, and with help from China as well as from its older friends, Pakistan again expanded its factory industries. It has also begun to extend its transportation and other service industries, and not only within the country. As examples, many foreign shipping companies are sending their vessels for repair and refitting in the big shipyards at Karachi. Pakistan has an international air service called Pakistan International Airlines.

But there is one problem which neither industrial progress nor higher standards of living can solve. If Pakistan is to play its part as a leading Muslim nation and one of the strongest developing nations it must have better relations with its huge neighbor India and its one-time partner Bangladesh. Pakistan took a welcome step by recognizing Bangladesh as a separate and independent nation. So the three nations need to decide that they can work together for the good of the subcontinent that they share and stop the tensions that are constantly between them. By working together, they could overcome their difficulties, and each could become more prosperous and play a fuller part in world affairs.

Another contrast seen in modern Pakistan. These men and the camel are standing near flares burning waste gas from a huge natural gas field. Pakistan today is trying to make use of all its natural resources to improve the economy of the country.

GLOSSARY

Buddha   Siddhartha Gautama, the founder of Buddhism

bullock   Young bull or steer

caste system   Social structure that divides people into various levels of privileges and abilities

chapatties   Thin unleavened pancakes

curry   Important spice to the Pakistani cuisine

gharry   Horsedrawn carriage used for transportation

Koran   Muslim equivalent of Christian bible

kulla   Skull cap worn by men under their turbans

minaret   Tower on Muslim mosques from which the call to prayer is given

purdah   Muslim belief that women should lead secluded lives, rarely going outside, and when they do they must be completely covered

shalwar   Baggy pajama-like pants

sherwani   Long, high collared coat

subcontinent   A major subdivision of a continent. The area including India and Pakistan is often referred to as the subcontinent (of Asia).

tonga   A cart pulled by a bullock used for transportation in the remoter regions

INDEX

Maurya Dynasty, 35
Mecca, 41, 81
Moguls, Mogul Dynasty, 11, 44, 46, 47, 54, 59, 61
Mohammed, 16, 41, 42, 81
Mohammedanism. *See* Islam
Mohenjo-Daro, 28
Muslim League, 63, 67
Muslims, 11, 16, 27, 41-44, 46, 47, 48, 49, 51, 57, 58, 61, 63, 64-65, 67, 68, 69, 70, 71, 81, 85

N

National Assembly, 74, 78
Nehru, Jawaharlal, 57, 62
Northwest Frontier Province, 25

P

Pathans, 93
Persians, 34
Peshawar, 92-93
Porus, King (India), 34
Potwar Plateau, 91
Punjab, 18, 20, 22, 25, 26, 30, 43, 84, 86
Punjabi, 26, 86
Purdah, 49, 85

R

Rahman, Sheikh Mujib ur, 78
Rainfall, 95
Ramadan, 81
Ravi River, 18, 22
Rawalpindi, 73, 91
Religion, 16, 27, 35-36, 38-40, 41-42, 51, 68, 69
Rivers, 18, 20, 22

104

S

Sanskrit, 10, 35, 50
Schools. *See* education
Scythians, 34
Sepoys, 58
Shah Jehan, 46
Shalimar Gardens, 92
Sharif, Mian, 79
Shiva, 36
Sikhs, 49, 55, 68
Sind, 22, 25, 26, 43, 86
Sindhi, 26, 86
Sofed Koh Mountains, 33
Spices, 52, 53, 54
Srinagar, 76
Sutlej River, 18, 22

T

Taj Mahal, 46
Tamerlane, 44
Thar (Indian) Desert, 22
Tirich Mir, Mount, 23
Tonga, 89
Turks, 11

U

United Nations Organization, 12
Untouchables, 37
Urdu, 26, 50, 72, 86-87

V

Vedas, 35
Vishnu, 36

Z

Zafar, Bahadur Shah, 59
Zia-ul-Haq, General, 13, 79